GAO
Accountability * Integrity * Reliability

Highlights

Highlights of GAO-12-711, a report to the Committee on Armed Services, U.S. Senate

FORCE STRUCTURE

Improved Cost Information and Analysis Needed to Guide Overseas Military Posture Decisions

I0430277

Why GAO Did This Study

In January 2012, DOD issued new strategic guidance on defense budget priorities, indicating that it must rebalance its overseas force posture— including the forward stationing of Navy ships in Spain for ballistic missile defense and the reduction of U.S. Army forces in Europe—in the face of deficit reduction. Similarly, DOD reported in its 2011 *Global Defense Posture Report to Congress* that savings associated with permanently stationing forces in the United States rather than overseas are often offset by such factors as increased rotational costs. Based on direction from the Senate Armed Services Committee, GAO evaluated the extent to which DOD has (1) conducted analysis to support recent overseas posture decisions and (2) developed a process for making posture decisions that align with strategy and consider costs. GAO assessed two recent posture initiatives, DOD plans and guidance related to posture, and theater posture plans from each combatant command.

What GAO Recommends

GAO recommends that DOD conduct a comprehensive cost analysis associated with the Navy's decision to station ships in Rota, assess options and costs related to rotating forces in Europe, and clarify roles and responsibilities of key entities to collect cost data on initiatives. DOD generally agreed with GAO's recommendations and identified corrective actions, but additional steps are needed to fully address GAO's recommendation that the Navy further assess options and costs for ballistic missile defense.

View GAO-12-711. For more information, contact John Pendleton at (404) 679-1816 or pendletonj@gao.gov.

What GAO Found

Although the Department of Defense (DOD) has conducted some analysis to support two recent global posture decisions, the full cost implications of these decisions are unknown.

- *Forward deployment and permanent stationing of U.S. Navy ships in Rota.* The Navy considered three options: (1) deploying ships to the region from U.S. bases, (2) forward stationing ships and crews overseas, and (3) deploying ships to the region and rotating crews from U.S. bases. The Navy concluded that forward stationing ships was the most efficient option, but GAO found that it did not fully consider the option to rotate crews from U.S. bases and, in a classified analysis, it used different assumptions for forward stationing versus deploying from the United States. These assumptions could affect the results of the analysis and have long-term cost implications. GAO's *Cost Estimating and Assessment Guide* states that a business case or cost-benefit analysis finds the best value solution by presenting facts and supporting details among competing alternatives, including the life cycle costs and benefits, and sensitivity to changes in assumptions. Without an analysis that controls for differing assumptions or considers factors such as complete life cycle costs, the long-term costs associated with its decision to forward station ships will remain unknown.

- *Reduction of U.S. Army force structure in Europe.* The planned reductions of U.S. Army forces in Europe will likely save money; however, decisions that could affect the extent of the savings are pending. For example, a 2010 Army analysis found $2 billion in savings over 10 years by returning forces from Germany, but assumed that new facilities estimated at $800 million would need to be built in the United States to house them. However, present planned reductions in overall Army end strength could eliminate the need for new construction. Further, DOD announced that it will rotate forces from the United States to Europe, but the nature of the rotations—which could include significant costs depending on their size and frequency—has not yet been defined. According to DOD officials, until such determinations are made, the savings to DOD will remain uncertain.

DOD has taken steps to align posture initiatives with strategy and cost, but continues to lack comprehensive and consistent cost estimates of initiatives. DOD's evolving posture process links initiatives with defense goals. Stakeholders from key DOD entities prioritize the initiatives in a voting process based on strategic criteria; cost is discussed, but not voted on. Furthermore, combatant commands did not completely and consistently report cost data in their theater posture plans because of the lack of readily available cost information. GAO found two primary reasons for this: unclear roles and responsibilities of key DOD organizations that have access to the cost data needed to compile and report comprehensive cost estimates and lack of a standardized format to compile and report cost data from component commands. Until these cost data are comprehensively compiled and reported, DOD and congressional decision makers will be unable to assess the true cost of posture initiatives.

_____ United States Government Accountability Office

The Department of the Interior protects and manages the nation's natural resources and cultural heritage; provides scientific and other information about those resources; and honors its special responsibilities to American Indians, Alaska Natives, and affiliated Island Communities.

NPS 612/112015, December 2011

www.ingramcontent.com/pod-product-compliance
Lightning Source LLC
Chambersburg PA
CBHW080749290526

45790CB00008B/3386

Contents

Abbreviations

DOD   Department of Defense
OSD   Office of the Secretary of Defense

This is a work of the U.S. government and is not subject to copyright protection in the United States. The published product may be reproduced and distributed in its entirety without further permission from GAO. However, because this work may contain copyrighted images or other material, permission from the copyright holder may be necessary if you wish to reproduce this material separately.

United States Government Accountability Office
Washington, DC 20548

June 6, 2012

The Honorable Carl Levin
Chairman
The Honorable John McCain
Ranking Member
Committee on Armed Services
United States Senate

In January 2012, the Department of Defense (DOD) issued new strategic guidance on defense budget priorities, indicating that it must rebalance its forces overseas in the face of the approaching end of a decade of war, a changing technological and geopolitical landscape, and the national security imperative of deficit reduction.[1] The same month, the administration announced a renewed strategic focus on the Asia-Pacific region and an adjustment of U.S. forces in Europe that included a decrease in permanently stationed forces while increasing the forces rotated temporarily to maintain presence and demonstrate commitment. Previously, the 2010 Quadrennial Defense Review highlighted the importance of periodically assessing and tailoring global defense posture in light of continued globalization and enduring transnational threats.[2] These recent changes are the latest in DOD's continuing efforts to do so.

This report is one in a series of GAO reports on DOD's global defense posture. Since 2006, we have reported on issues related to DOD's overall global posture strategy and management practices, the military buildup on Guam, the transformation of Army posture in Europe, and the establishment of U.S. Africa Command.[3] Those reports contain a number of recommendations to improve DOD's management of these efforts and to enhance the information that DOD makes available about them to

---

[1] DOD, *Sustaining U.S. Global Leadership: Priorities for 21st Century Defense* (Washington, D.C.: Jan. 3, 2012).

[2] In DOD's 2010 Quadrennial Defense Review, DOD identified global defense posture as (1) forward stationed and rotationally deployed forces, capabilities, and equipment; (2) a supporting overseas network of infrastructure and facilities; and (3) a series of treaty, access, transit and status-protection agreements and arrangements with allies and key partners.

[3] GAO, *Defense Management: Additional Cost Information and Stakeholder Input Needed to Assess Military Posture in Europe*, GAO-11-131 (Washington, D.C.: Feb. 3, 2011).

GAO-12-711 Force Structure

decision makers in the executive branch and Congress. In many cases, DOD has agreed with our recommendations and has taken actions to implement them. A list of these related products is included at the end of this report.

Congressional committees have also taken several actions in recent years that emphasize the need for DOD to consider fiscal constraints in defense planning. For example, the Senate Armed Services Committee report accompanying a proposed bill for the National Defense Authorization Act for Fiscal Year 2012 directed DOD to update the committee on its plans to implement GAO's previous recommendations to more accurately and comprehensively account for costs related to theater posture plans.[4] The committee report also directed GAO to assess the methodology and assumptions behind the assertion DOD made in its 2011 *Global Defense Posture Report to Congress* that savings associated with permanently stationing forces in the United States rather than overseas are often offset by such factors as increased rotational costs. Consequently, this report examines the extent to which DOD has (1) conducted an analysis of costs and savings associated with recent overseas posture decisions and (2) developed a process for making decisions about global posture initiatives that align with strategy and consider costs, as well as efforts made by combatant commands to compile and report comprehensive cost data on both existing global posture and new initiatives in their theater posture plans.

To determine the extent to which DOD conducted analysis of costs and savings associated with recent overseas posture decisions, we reviewed DOD documented cost data and collected additional information by interviewing officials associated with two major global force posture initiatives that DOD officials identified to support its conclusion that cost savings associated with permanently stationing forces in the United States rather than overseas are often offset by such factors as increased rotational costs: the stationing of four Navy destroyers in Rota, Spain, to provide ballistic missile defense for the region and the reduction of permanently stationed Army forces in Europe. To determine the extent to which DOD conducted analysis to support the decision to station four Navy destroyers in Rota, Spain, we analyzed key documents and briefings provided by the U.S. Navy, U.S. European Command, and

---

[4] *See* S. Rep. No. 112-26, at 191-92 (2011).

Naval Station Rota; conducted a site visit to Naval Station Rota; and interviewed officials from the U.S. Navy, Office of the Chief of Naval Operations; U.S. European Command; U.S. Navy Europe; and Naval Station Rota. To determine the extent to which DOD conducted analysis to support Army force structure reductions in Europe, we conducted a site visit to Germany; reviewed key documents from U.S. European Command and U.S. Army Europe that describe the status of planned force structure changes in Europe, including U.S. European Command's 2010 and 2011 theater posture plans; and interviewed officials from the Office of the Secretary of Defense (OSD); OSD Cost Assessment and Program Evaluation; Office of the Under Secretary of Defense (Comptroller); Department of the Army, Program Assessment and Evaluation Division; U.S. European Command; and U.S. Army Europe. We also analyzed and assessed cost estimates for several courses of action associated with the number of Army brigade combat teams in Europe developed by the U.S. Army, Program Assessment and Evaluation Division, against our cost estimating criteria to determine the extent to which Army analysts employed best practices when developing the estimates.

To determine the extent to which DOD has a process in place for making decisions about global posture initiatives that aligns with strategy and considers costs, including progress made by combatant commands to compile and report comprehensive cost data on existing posture and new initiatives in their theater posture plans, we evaluated core global posture strategy documents, current and draft DOD guidance, and other documentation we collected through interviews with officials from OSD; the Joint Staff; U.S. European Command and its three service component commands; U.S. Pacific Command; U.S. Africa Command; the four service headquarters; OSD Cost Assessment and Program Evaluation; the Office of the Under Secretary of Defense (Comptroller); and the Office of Under Secretary of Defense for Acquisition, Technology and Logistics. We also observed the Joint Staff's November 2011 Posture Review Seminar and analyzed and evaluated theater posture plans from 2010 and 2011 for each combatant command.

We conducted this performance audit between June 2011 and May 2012 in accordance with generally accepted government auditing standards. Those standards require that we plan and perform the audit to obtain sufficient, appropriate evidence to provide a reasonable basis for our findings and conclusions based on our audit objectives. We believe that the evidence obtained provides a reasonable basis for our findings and conclusions based on our audit objectives. Appendix I provides a more detailed description of our scope and methodology.

Background

DOD operates six geographic combatant commands, each with an assigned area of responsibility (see fig. 1). Each geographic combatant command carries out a variety of missions and activities, including humanitarian assistance and combat operations, and assigns functions to subordinate commanders. Each command is supported by a service component command from each of the services and by a theater special operations command. The Departments of the Army, Navy, and Air Force have key roles in making decisions on where to locate their forces when they are not otherwise employed or deployed by order of the Secretary of Defense or assigned to a combatant command. In addition, the military departments allocate budgetary resources to construct, maintain, and repair buildings, structures, and utilities and to acquire the real property or interests in real property necessary to carry out their responsibilities. Together, the combatant commands and service component commands develop theater posture plans that seek to prioritize force structure changes and posture initiatives that will best meet national security and strategic priorities for a given area of responsibility.

Figure 1: Geographic Combatant Command Areas of Responsibility

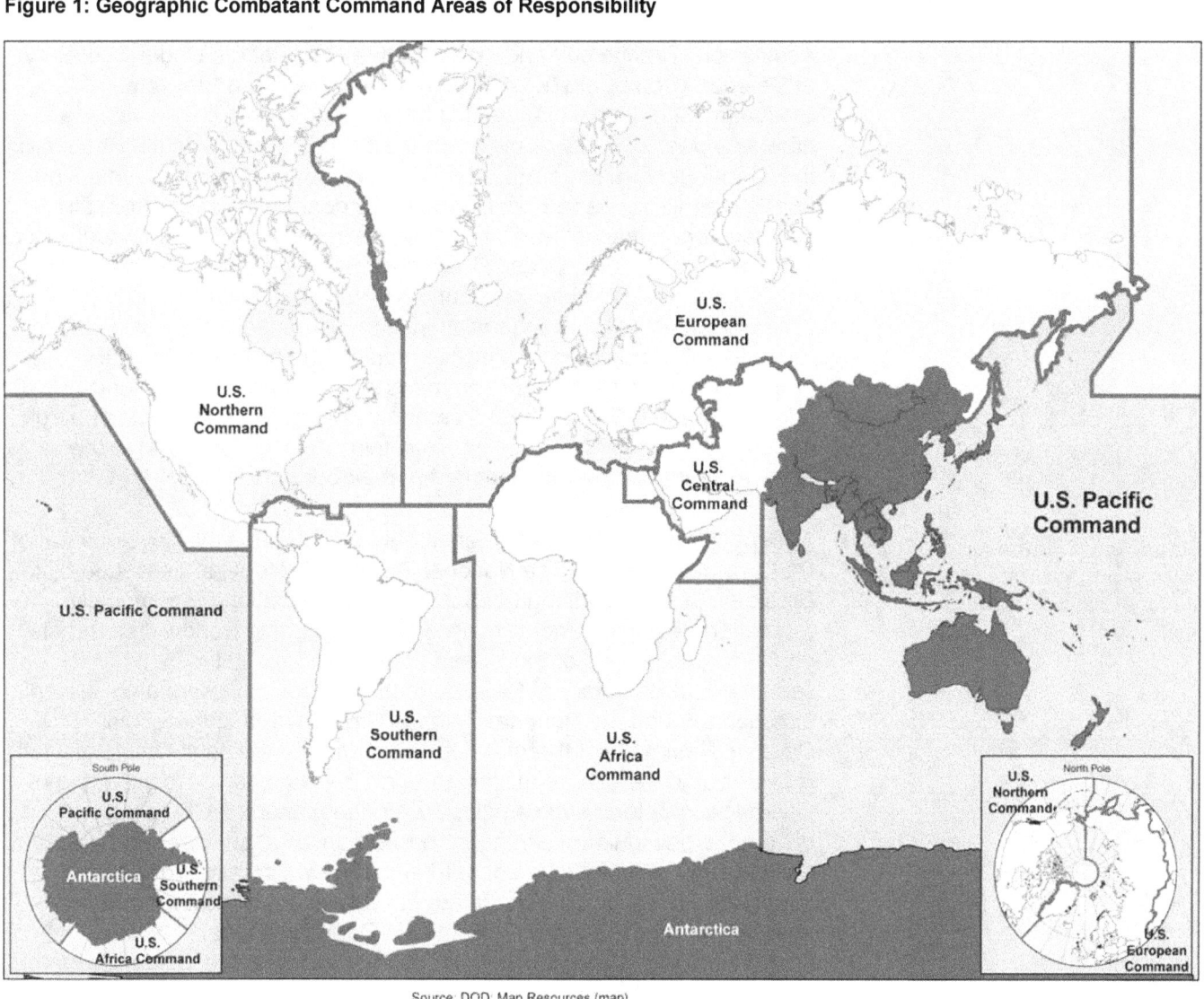

Source: DOD; Map Resources (map).

The process for assessing global posture initiatives is managed under the framework of the Global Posture Executive Council, which consists of representatives from the military services, the combatant commands, the Joint Staff, and OSD. The purpose of the Global Posture Executive Council includes facilitating senior leader posture decision making and overseeing the assessment and implementation of posture plans. The Principal Deputy Under Secretary of Defense for Policy and the Director, Joint Staff, serve as co-chairmen of the council, and its membership includes senior representatives from both offices, as well as representatives from the Office of the Under Secretary of Defense for Acquisition, Technology and Logistics; the Office of the Under Secretary of Defense (Comptroller); OSD Cost Assessment and Program Evaluation; the Joint Staff; the combatant commands; the services; and others as needed. Subordinate to the Global Posture Executive Council is the Global Posture Integration Team, which consists of representatives from each military department who review posture initiatives from all combatant commands' theater posture plans included in the annual global posture prioritization process. The prioritization process itself takes place in a 3-day seminar held in or around November of each year during which 22 representatives from organizations that comprise the Global Posture Executive Council come together to review the posture initiatives proposed in each combatant command's theater posture plan and prioritize these initiatives based primarily on how they align with strategic defense guidance. The prioritized initiatives are then provided to the services to inform the development of their budgets.[5]

A hierarchy of national and defense guidance informs the development of DOD's global posture. The National Security Strategy, to be issued by the President at the beginning of each new administration, and annually thereafter, describes and discusses topics including worldwide interests, goals, and objectives of the United States that are vital to its national security. The Secretary of Defense then provides corresponding strategic direction through the National Defense Strategy and Quadrennial Defense Reviews. Furthermore, the Chairman of the Joint Chiefs of Staff provides guidance to the military through the National Military Strategy. On specific matters, such as global defense posture, DOD has also developed new guidance in numerous documents, principally the 2010 Guidance for the Employment of the Force—which consolidates and integrates planning guidance related to operations and other military activities—and the 2010 Joint Strategic Capabilities Plan—which implements the strategic policy direction provided in the Guidance for the Employment of the Force. The Joint Strategic Capabilities Plan also tasks combatant commanders to develop theater campaign, contingency, and posture plans that are consistent with the Guidance for the Employment

---

[5] The posture prioritization process focuses on new overseas military construction-related initiatives identified in the combatant commands' theater posture plans.

of the Force.[6] The theater campaign plan translates strategic objectives to facilitate the development of operational and contingency plans, while the theater posture plan provides an overview of posture requirements to support those plans and identifies major ongoing and new posture initiatives to address capability gaps, including current and planned military construction requirements. Figure 2 illustrates the relationships among these national and DOD strategic guidance documents.

Figure 2: National and DOD Guidance, Strategies, and Plans Related to Global Defense Posture

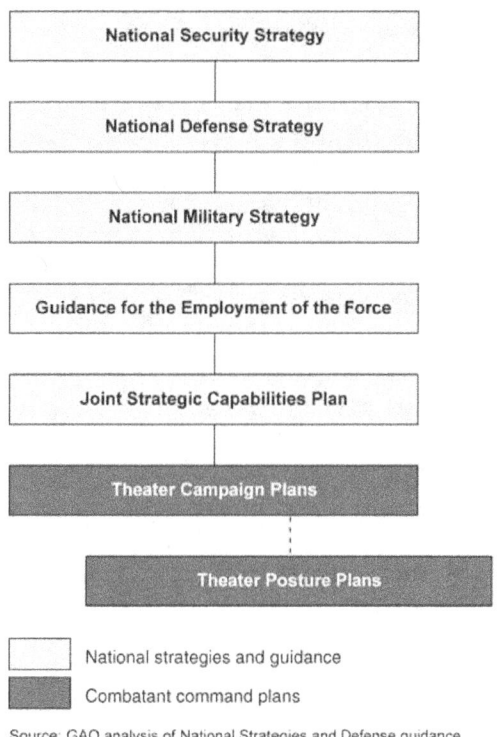

National strategies and guidance

Combatant command plans

Source: GAO analysis of National Strategies and Defense guidance.

---

[6] Currently, functional combatant commands and U.S. Northern Command are not required to submit theater posture plans but provide similar information in a different format.

We have issued a number of related reports about force structure and global force posture planning. In February 2011, we reported that U.S. European Command lacks comprehensive cost data in its theater posture plans and therefore decision makers lack critical information that could be used to make fully informed posture decisions.[7] We recommended, therefore, that DOD revise its posture planning guidance to require comprehensive cost estimates of posture costs and provide for consistent analysis of posture alternatives. In May 2011, we reported that DOD was transforming the facilities and infrastructure that support its posture in Asia without the benefit of comprehensive cost information or an analysis of alternatives and recommended that DOD develop a business case analysis for its Korea tour normalization initiative and that it develop comprehensive costs estimates for posture initiatives in the Pacific as a whole.[8] Finally, in April 2010, we reported that U.S. Africa Command had not yet finalized decisions related to force presence and structure in Africa, including the Combined Joint Task Force-Horn of Africa at Camp Lemonnier, Djibouti.[9] We recommended that the command complete an evaluation of the task force and determine its future, to include a long-term activity assessment, a funding plan, and training guidance. DOD generally agreed with these recommendations and has taken some steps to implement them.

The Cost Implications of Evolving Plans for Overseas Presence Are Uncertain

Although DOD has conducted some analysis to support recent global defense posture decisions, the cost implications of these decisions are unknown. In its 2011 *Global Defense Posture Report to Congress*, DOD asserted that cost savings associated with permanently stationing forces in the United States rather than overseas are offset by other factors, such as increased costs to periodically rotate forces back to overseas locations. To support this assertion, OSD identified two posture initiatives: (1) the forward deployment and permanent stationing of U.S. Navy ships in Rota, Spain, in support of ballistic missile defense and (2) the reduction of U.S. Army force structure in Europe. Based on our review of the

---

[7] GAO-11-131.

[8] GAO, *Defense Management: Comprehensive Cost Information and Analysis of Alternatives Needed to Assess Military Posture in Asia*, GAO-11-316 (Washington, D.C.: May 25, 2011).

[9] GAO, *Defense Management: DOD Needs to Determine the Future of Its Horn of Africa Task Force*, GAO-10-504 (Washington, D.C.: Apr. 15, 2010).

analysis behind these two posture initiatives, we found that the analysis supporting the first was incomplete and that any analysis of the second cannot be completed until several basic decisions are made and assumptions defined.

Decision to Forward Station Ships in Europe Could Allow the Navy to Provide Missile Defense with Fewer Ships, but the Long-Term Costs Are Not Well Defined

The Secretary of the Navy recently announced the permanent stationing of four Aegis-equipped ships in Rota, Spain—two ships in fiscal year 2014 and the other two ships in fiscal year 2015—in order to more efficiently address the operational requirements associated with the President's Phased Adaptive Approach for European ballistic missile defense.[10]

The Navy considered and compared three options in order to determine the most appropriate way to address the operational requirements for ballistic missile defense in Europe: (1) deploying ships to the region from U.S. bases, (2) forward stationing ships and crews within the U.S. European Command area of responsibility, and (3) deploying ships to the region and rotating crews from U.S. bases. The Navy concluded that forward stationing ships represented the most efficient and strategically beneficial of the three options. We reviewed the Navy's documentation associated with the decision and found two key issues. First, the Navy did not fully consider the rotational crewing option. Second, the Navy used different operational assumptions for the remaining two options and did not control for those differences prior to comparing the analytical results.

- *Limited analysis of the rotational crewing option.* The Navy provided little documentation for its analysis of the option to forward station ships and rotate crews from U.S. bases—also known as rotational crewing. This option avoids permanently relocating ship crews and their families. Navy officials stated that rotational crewing was undesirable because of its deleterious effect on crew efficiency and morale. Our previous reports found that the Navy had not developed comprehensive guidance for implementing rotational crewing initiatives or a systemic approach for analyzing rotational crewing

---

[10] According to DOD's 2010 Ballistic Missile Defense Review Report, the European Phased Adaptive Approach represents DOD's plan to adopt a new regionally based approach to delivering ballistic missile defense. The report states that the administration is committed to implementing the new European Phased Adaptive Approach and sees it as the U.S. national contribution to a NATO missile defense capability.

GAO-12-711 Force Structure

alternatives and lessons learned. Moreover, as we reported in 2008, initial Navy rotational crewing efforts had provided greater forward presence for Navy ships by eliminating ship transits and maintaining more on-station time in distant operating areas.[11] Therefore, a rotational crewing approach for this posture decision could potentially provide a strategically effective and cost-effective option. However, the Navy provided less analysis of this option than the other two options, which may have prevented the Navy from determining the potential operational value of this approach.

- *Different operational assumptions not controlled for in analysis of alternatives.* The Navy provided more documentation and analysis for its comparison of the forward stationing option to the current approach of U.S.-based deployments to the region. As a result of its analysis, the Navy concluded that the forward stationing option requires significantly fewer ships to meet European ballistic missile defense mission requirements and therefore represents the more efficient and cost-effective option. However, we found that the Navy applied different assumptions to the two options and did not demonstrate that it had controlled for those differences, both of which could affect the outcome of the analysis.[12] Further, Navy officials did not demonstrate that they had considered the long-term life cycle effect and associated costs for each forward deployed ship. Such factors may represent significant costs, without which DOD may lack the comprehensive analysis needed to determine the most efficient approach for meeting ballistic missile defense mission requirements.

GAO's *Cost Estimating and Assessment Guide* states that a business case analysis or a cost-benefit analysis seeks to find the best value solution by linking each alternative to how it satisfies a strategic objective. This linkage is achieved by developing business cases that present facts and supporting details among competing alternatives, including the life cycle costs and quantifiable and nonquantifiable benefits. Specifically, each alternative should identify (1) relative life cycle costs and benefits;

---

[11] GAO, *Force Structure: Navy Needs to Fully Evaluate Options and Provide Standard Guidance for Implementing Surface Ship Rotational Crewing*, GAO-05-10 (Washington, D.C.: Nov. 10, 2004), and *Force Structure: Ship Rotational Crewing Initiatives Would Benefit from Top-Level Leadership, Navy-wide Guidance, Comprehensive Analysis, and Improved Lessons-Learned Sharing*, GAO-08-418 (Washington, D.C.: May 29, 2008).

[12] The specifics of the assumptions are classified and are therefore not included in this report.

(2) methods and rationale for quantifying the life cycle costs and benefits; (3) effect and value of cost, schedule, and performance trade-offs; (4) sensitivity to changes in assumptions; and (5) risk factors. Finally, the analysis should be unbiased, consider all possible alternatives, and be rigorous enough that independent auditors can review it and clearly understand why a particular alternative was chosen. DOD guidance regarding economic analysis similarly encourages the use of sensitivity analysis, a tool that can be used to determine the extent to which costs and benefits change or are sensitive to changes in key factors; this analysis can produce a range of costs and benefits that may provide a better guide or indicator than a single estimate.[13]

In contrast, the Navy's choice to forward station ships in Europe was informed by cost and strategic factors. The Navy considered a number of basing options in or near the Mediterranean and developed a decision matrix that included both strategic and cost factors, such as the proximity of each site to the planned deployment regions and the amount of military construction that would be required at each site to support the ships and their crews. Based on these factors, Navy officials determined that Naval Station Rota provided the best option. From a strategic and operational perspective, Naval Station Rota provides the U.S. Navy with a large maritime port and an associated airfield close to current and potential future operating areas. Additionally, since it is a home port for the Spanish Navy and currently houses Spanish military ships of similar size, there is no need to expand the port pier space to accommodate the incoming ships. Figure 3 shows the current port pier space.

---

[13] *See* Department of Defense Instruction 7041.3, *Economic Analysis for Decisionmaking*, enc. A, attachment 1 (Nov. 7, 1995).

Figure 3: Current Port Pier Space at Naval Station Rota

Source: DOD.

While Naval Station Rota can accommodate the expanded mission, some costs will be incurred. The infrastructure at Rota was initially designed to accommodate a much larger contingent of military personnel and family members than it does currently. Its capacity, according to Navy officials, is sufficient to accommodate the personnel numbers expected once the ships, their crews, and the crews' families are stationed there. As such, although some military construction will be required, less would be required at Rota than at any of the other sites in the U.S. European Command area of responsibility that were considered. Specifically, the Navy estimated it would cost approximately $33 million for construction of new facilities and upgrades to existing infrastructure. Further, Naval Station Rota officials explained, and we observed, that the base currently has sufficient galley, medical, and housing facilities and that there are no plans to expand the physical footprint of on-base support infrastructure. The Navy also considered estimated up-front and recurring increases in operational and personnel expenses, including those for additional support personnel and increased utilities costs. In total, the Navy estimated that it would incur approximately $166 million in up-front military construction, personnel, and maintenance costs; an annual increase in operations and maintenance; and personnel costs of approximately $179 million.[14]

DOD Will Likely Save Money by Reducing Army Forces and Headquarters in Europe, but Amount of Savings Depends on Future Decisions

To save money, and consistent with a shift in strategic emphasis toward the Asia-Pacific region, the Secretary of Defense announced plans in January 2012 to reduce U.S. Army forces in Europe. The announced reductions include the removal of two heavy brigade combat teams, a corps headquarters, and various combat support and service support units, and would affect about 10,000 soldiers and their families. U.S. Army Europe officials told us that the reductions should be completed by 2015. The department's actions are consistent with a GAO recommendation in 2010 that DOD consider alternatives for its European posture plans in part because the Army's analysis indicated that such a reduction could potentially save $2 billion over 10 years.[15] However, several decisions are pending or have recently been made that could affect the ultimate savings to DOD. These are as follows:

- *Overall Army force structure.* The Army's 2010 analysis that found up to $2 billion in savings over 10 years from returning forces from Germany also assumed that more than $800 million in military construction funds would be needed to construct new facilities in the United States should two brigade combat teams be returned to the United States.[16] However, the Army announced in February 2012 that the 170th brigade combat team stationed in Baumholder, Germany, and the 172nd brigade combat team stationed in Grafenwoehr,

---

[14] These cost estimates include increases in infrastructure, personnel, training, and maintenance.

[15] GAO, *Defense Planning: DOD Needs to Review the Costs and Benefits of Basing Alternatives for Army Forces in Europe*, GAO-10-745R (Washington, D.C.: Sept. 13, 2010).

[16] The 10-year time period identified in the analysis is fiscal years 2012 through 2021.

Germany, will be eliminated from Army force structure in fiscal years 2013 and 2014, respectively, as part of the larger end strength reductions. Given this force structure reduction, the savings to the Army and DOD could be billions more because the costs of manning and equipping two brigade combat teams (with approximately 4,000 personnel each), among other units, would no longer be incurred. For example, past GAO work has found that annual compensation costs exceed $125,000 per active duty soldier; removing two brigade combat teams from the Army would reduce personnel costs by about $1 billion annually.[17] Furthermore, the $800 million assumed in military construction funds needed to construct new facilities from the 2010 analysis is no longer likely to be needed.

- *Consolidation of U.S. Army Europe headquarters functions remaining in Germany.* The consolidation of headquarters for U.S. Army Europe, 5th Signal Command, and a military intelligence brigade in Wiesbaden permits the closure of communities in Mannheim, Heidelberg, and Darmstadt. According to U.S. Army Europe, this consolidation effort—which eliminates 47 sites, 9 schools, and 3 sets of community support infrastructure[18]—will provide an estimated annual recurring savings of $112 million. The savings from these consolidations would be in addition to the approximately $2 billion associated with removing the brigade combat teams from Europe forecasted by the Army's 2010 analysis.[19]

- *Potential increase in special operations forces in Europe.* In January 2012, the Secretary of Defense also announced plans to increase special operations forces stationed in Europe. However, the type and size of those forces have not yet been determined. Officials from U.S. Army Europe told us that they are considering locations to station special operations forces and thereby realize efficiencies through

---

[17] The average total compensation per active duty servicemember includes items such as cash compensation and allowances (basic pay/housing), noncash benefits (health care/education), and deferred benefits (retirement pay/veterans affairs health care).

[18] According to DOD officials, examples of community support infrastructure include post exchanges, health care centers, and spousal career centers.

[19] U.S. European Command officials told us they are currently implementing the decision to consolidate bases at Wiesbaden and that any estimated savings will not be fully realized until the consolidation effort is complete.

consolidation, but that they cannot move forward on this until they know the requirements for the increase in special operations forces.

- *Decision about U.S. Africa Command headquarters location.*[20] In 2008, DOD formed a new combatant command to focus on Africa. That command was located in temporary facilities in Stuttgart, Germany—also home to U.S. European Command—pending decisions about where to locate it permanently. Initially, DOD had planned to place the command somewhere in Africa but could not find a suitable location after encountering resistance from potential African partners. In 2009, GAO recommended that DOD conduct an assessment to determine where U.S. Africa Command would be permanently located and, until that time, limit expenditures on temporary headquarters infrastructure.[21] However, these decisions had not been made; officials from U.S. Africa Command told us in February 2012 that OSD Cost Assessment and Program Evaluation is conducting a study to assess the risks and cost implications associated with relocating the headquarters in the United States that should be completed by mid-2012.

- *Rotational force plans.* DOD has also announced its intent to periodically rotate Army forces from the United States to supplement the two Army brigade combat teams that will remain in Europe and thus show commitment to European allies. However, according to U.S. European Command officials, the size and frequency of the rotations—which could include significant costs—have not yet been defined, and until there is a determination of the size of the forces that will be rotated to Europe and the frequency at which they will be rotated, any estimation of the cost or cost savings will remain uncertain. According to the Army's 2010 analysis, it would potentially cost the Army approximately $1 billion over 10 years to rotate two brigade combat teams to Europe twice per year, which would allow the United States to maintain its current presence but would offset the savings garnered by reductions in the overall force structure. However, Army officials told us that they did not think that rotating

---

[20] Although this decision pertains to a combatant command, funding for the installation containing the command's headquarters is included in the Army's budget.

[21] GAO, *Defense Management: Actions Needed to Address Stakeholder Concerns, Improve Interagency Collaboration, and Determine Full Costs Associated with the U.S. Africa Command*, GAO-09-181 (Washington, D.C.: Feb. 20, 2009).

entire brigades was likely and that they were currently examining options, including rotating smaller formations, such as companies or battalion-sized elements. The potential rotations will likely have implications on the final basing plan in Europe as well, as the Army would likely want to maintain facilities in Europe for rotating forces.

Until the decisions outlined above are made—especially regarding the plans to rotate forces back to Europe—the full extent of the savings that will be realized in light of the Secretary of Defense's January 2012 decision to reduce the size of permanently stationed U.S. Army forces in Europe will remain uncertain. Based on previous GAO and Army analysis, there is the potential for DOD to save considerably more than the $2 billion originally estimated in light of DOD's decision to remove the brigades from the force structure. Looking forward, the decisions about the size and frequency of Army rotations will be a key cost driver. Costs will be incurred not only to pay for the rotations, but assumptions about these rotations will also be used to decide which Army installations in Europe to retain.

DOD Has Taken Steps to Align Posture Initiatives with Strategy and Cost but Continues to Lack Comprehensive and Consistent Cost Estimates of Initiatives

DOD's Process to Prioritize Posture Initiatives Is Improving

In part to respond to previous GAO recommendations,[22] DOD recognized the need to prioritize initiatives to reflect strategic goals, has taken steps to align posture initiatives with defense strategy, and has begun to gather cost information. DOD's evolving global defense posture process links posture initiatives with defense goals and prioritizes those initiatives based on strategic and implementation criteria. Strategic criteria are defined by four focus areas: enabling crisis response, ensuring access for global posture enablers, shaping and improving security cooperation, and supporting contingencies and ongoing operations. Implementation criteria include such factors as operational flexibility, operational management and institutional provisions of the force, ease of implementation, and international relations. Based on our observation of the process, all posture initiatives submitted by combatant commands in their theater posture plans are discussed and voted on within the framework of the strategic and implementation criteria by 22 stakeholders from the Global Posture Executive Council using electronic voting software displayed on a projection screen. The result is a list of posture initiatives ranked in order of strategic priority. During the process, the stakeholders also discuss the approximate costs associated with each initiative, but cost is not considered a key factor and is not voted on. According to DOD officials, this is because costs are considered both before and after the prioritization process (before by the combatant command and after by the

---

[22] GAO, *Force Structure: Actions Needed to Improve DOD's Ability to Manage, Assess, and Report on Global Defense Posture Initiatives*, GAO-09-706R (Washington, D.C.: July 2, 2009).

services in their budget processes) and because the costs associated with an initiative are always discussed before voting takes place.

Combatant Commands Reported Some Cost Data in Their 2011 Theater Posture Plans, but Gaps Remain

Although the geographic combatant commands are responsible for reporting cost data on existing global posture, we found that the combatant commands did not completely and consistently report cost data in their 2011 theater posture plans. Our prior work has demonstrated, however, that comprehensive cost information is a key component in enabling decision makers to set funding priorities, develop annual budget requests, and evaluate resource requirements at key decision points.[23] Specifically, GAO previously recommended that DOD should compile and report comprehensive cost data in the combatant commands' theater posture plans.[24] DOD officials told us that in response to this recommendation, DOD revised an enclosure in the 2010 Joint Strategic Capabilities Plan to direct the combatant commands to include the following cost data on current posture in their theater posture plans:

- ongoing, current year, and 5-year planned posture initiatives listed by title and cost;
- full project costs, that is, construction costs plus furniture, fixtures, equipment, and any operation and maintenance costs;
- implementation progress (when appropriate); and
- host nation participation (when appropriate).

Despite this guidance, our review of the 2011 theater posture plans submitted by the five geographic combatant commands found that though all of them partially complied with the revised guidance, none met all the requirements.[25] For example, some theater posture plans included current year cost data but no cost data for the out years. Additionally, some theater posture plans did not report key cost data, such as military construction costs or operation and maintenance costs. Three of the five posture plans did not include implementation progress for each initiative and did not indicate why this information was not included.

---

[23] GAO-11-316.

[24] GAO-11-131.

[25] We reviewed classified theater posture plans from the five combatant commands required to submit them—U.S. Africa Command, U.S. Central Command, U.S. European Command, U.S. Pacific Command, and U.S. Southern Command.

Additionally, DOD published supplemental guidance in early 2011 that directs the combatant commands to provide initiative summary sheets for each new posture initiative in their 2011 theater posture plans. These summary sheets are used to inform the prioritization process and include several elements, such as approximate costs broken out by fiscal year and host nation funding (if known), for each posture initiative. However, we found that cost data were not consistently reported in the initiative summary sheets for new posture initiatives as accurately as possible. Therefore, cost data for new posture initiatives may not be able to be accurately compared during the prioritization process. DOD officials told us that in the months between issuance of the theater posture plans and the prioritization process, combatant commands have the opportunity to provide updated cost information for new initiatives.

Based on our analysis as well as remarks from DOD officials involved in the process, there are two reasons that combatant commands have not been able to accurately and consistently report cost information for their posture initiatives. The first is the lack of clarity about roles and responsibilities. Joint doctrine discussing the components of a joint force notes the responsibility of service component commanders to develop program and budget requests that comply with combatant commander guidance on warfighting requirements and priorities.[26] In addition, the doctrine states that component commanders will provide a copy of the program submission to the combatant commander prior to forwarding it to the service headquarters, and will keep the combatant commander informed of the status of combatant command requirements while service programs are under development. However, according to OSD officials, the combatant commands did not have access to comprehensive cost data that they were required to compile and report because some of the data are compiled by service component commands and the military departments. Officials we interviewed from three combatant commands echoed this sentiment, explaining that while the combatant command is responsible for developing mission requirements for its respective region, it is the military departments that are responsible for developing the budgets that fund initiatives meant to address mission requirements. OSD officials told us that in order to address this lack of clarity over roles and responsibilities, OSD has drafted a DOD instruction outlining the U.S.

---

[26] Joint Chiefs of Staff, Joint Pub. 1, *Doctrine for the Armed Forces of the United States* (May 2, 2007) (incorporating change Mar. 20, 2009).

global defense posture process, which includes specific guidance to the combatant commands and military departments on providing cost data associated with new posture initiatives. Additionally, OSD officials told us that they are in the process of promulgating a data call to issue to the military departments and combatant commands to facilitate determination of the cost of current overseas posture. Key OSD organizations involved in these efforts include OSD Cost Assessment and Program Evaluation; the Office of the Under Secretary of Defense for Policy; the Office of the Under Secretary of Defense (Comptroller); and the Office of the Under Secretary of Defense for Acquisition, Technology and Logistics. We were unable to evaluate the instruction, however, because it was under continuous revision and had not been finalized during the time of our review.

The second reason that combatant commands have not been able to accurately and consistently report cost information for their posture initiatives is the lack of a standardized format with which to report the information. Current DOD guidance does not provide a standardized format for the combatant commands to use when requesting information from service component commands, in order to consistently report the required cost data for each posture initiative. Accordingly, officials from U.S. Army Europe and U.S. Air Force Europe stated, for example, that requests for cost data are either too broad or too vague and that fulfilling these data requests is labor intensive. Without a standardized format for reporting cost information associated with each global posture initiative, decision makers on the Global Posture Executive Council cannot accurately consider and compare costs associated with different initiatives.

Conclusions

By asserting that cost savings associated with decreasing overseas presence are often offset through costs incurred and operational impacts elsewhere, DOD has tempered expectations for savings associated with such reductions. However, in an increasingly constrained budget era, DOD and congressional decision makers need precise estimates so that they can more readily balance resources against strategic requirements. To this end, estimates associated with global posture decisions should be backed by rigorous analysis based on information that is as complete and comprehensive as possible. The potential costs or cost savings that may arise from recent posture decisions in the U.S. European Command area of responsibility will remain uncertain without additional analysis. Specifically, the decision to forward station Aegis-equipped ships at Naval Station Rota may allow the Navy to meet the ballistic mission with fewer ships overall but could cost DOD approximately $1 billion over a 5-year period. And, until a more rigorous analysis of the decision is conducted, the costs of the other options considered will remain unknown. Further, costs and cost savings associated with the decision to reduce Army forces in Europe and adjust the Army's basing footprint in the region will remain unknown until options related to rotational forces and their associated costs are identified and assessed.

At a department wide level, DOD has taken positive steps to develop a process for prioritizing posture initiatives. Currently, the process considers, but is not driven by, cost. However, it remains essential that comprehensive cost information for each initiative be compiled and reported so that once initiatives are proposed, they can be adequately prioritized, resourced, and approved. The current process is hampered by the inconsistency with which cost data are reported; the lack of clarity on the roles and responsibilities of key OSD organizations, military departments, combatant commands, and service component commands in helping to develop these cost estimates; and the lack of any standardized template with which to report them. Lacking this information, department and congressional decision makers will be unable to adequately assess the true cost of global posture initiatives in the future.

Recommendations for Executive Action

To identify future funding requirements and improve the posture planning process, we recommend that the Secretary of Defense take the following three actions:

- Direct the Secretary of the Navy to conduct a comprehensive analysis for each course of action the Navy has considered to address mission requirements for ballistic missile defense in the Mediterranean that compares all options the Navy considered and either applies consistent operational assumptions or controls for different operational assumptions and includes the long-term life cycle costs and annual operating costs associated with forward stationing.
- Direct the Secretary of the Army to identify and assess options to rotate forces in Europe and their associated costs, including the impacts on future basing in Europe.
- Clarify the roles and responsibilities of key OSD organizations, the military departments, and the service component commands, and establish a standardized reporting format to include in applicable guidance for key DOD organizations to use to ensure that cost information is consistently summarized and reported to inform the posture planning process.

Agency Comments and Our Evaluation

In written comments on a draft of this report, DOD generally agreed with our recommendations and has already initiated certain actions to address them. DOD's response acknowledged that conducting analysis prior to making posture decisions is important, and that the actions it has taken or plans to take should provide a greater understanding of the global defense posture process and its consideration of costs. However, we believe some additional steps are warranted in order to fully address our recommendations.

In response to our recommendation that the Secretary of Defense direct the Secretary of the Navy to conduct a comprehensive analysis for each course of action the Navy has considered to address mission requirements for ballistic missile defense in the Mediterranean, that compares all options the Navy considered and either applies consistent operational assumptions or controls for different operational assumptions and includes the long-term life cycle costs and annual operating costs associated with forward stationing, DOD partially concurred, but did not identify additional actions to address the recommendation. Specifically, DOD agreed that analysis should be conducted prior to making posture decisions, but does not agree that additional analysis is needed to support the decision to forward station four ships in Rota, Spain. As discussed in this report, we acknowledge that the Navy conducted some analysis to support this decision, including the development and consideration of some estimated costs, but we found the analysis inconsistent and incomplete. For example, while the Navy initially stated that it considered rotational crewing as an option, we found its analysis was limited when compared to the other options. In its written comments, DOD identified concerns with this approach, including increased stress on the crews; however, the analysis supporting the decision did not include a discussion of these issues. Additionally, we found that the Navy did not control for the different assumptions used to develop the ship number requirements associated with the forward stationing and U.S.-based deployment approaches, which could have altered the results of the analysis and could represent significant long-term costs. If the Navy maintains that forward stationing is the most effective and efficient means to meet the ballistic missile defense requirement in Europe, DOD would still benefit from determining the life cycle costs associated with the decision in order to determine its true long-term costs, which could be significant. While DOD provided onetime capital costs and average yearly operations and maintenance costs for this option, it remains unclear whether these are long-term life cycle cost estimates. Based on our findings and our cost estimating guide that states that a credible business case analysis should include life cycle costs as well as quantifiable and nonquantifiable benefits, we maintain that the Navy, DOD, and Congress would benefit from additional analysis in order to develop a more comprehensive cost estimate associated with the decision to forward station ships in Rota.

DOD agreed with our recommendation that the Secretary of Defense direct the Secretary of the Army to identify and assess options to rotate forces in Europe and their associated costs, including the impacts on future basing in Europe, and stated that certain actions are ongoing. Specifically, the Army is currently working with U.S. European Command and various Army components to identify and assess options for rotating personnel and equipment through Europe for training and exercises with allies and partners. If fully implemented, we believe DOD's actions should meet the intent of our recommendation.

DOD also agreed with our recommendation to clarify the roles and responsibilities of key OSD organizations, the military departments, and the service component commands, and establish a standardized reporting format that will be included in applicable guidance for key DOD organizations to use to ensure that cost information is consistently summarized and reported to inform the posture planning process, and stated that certain actions are under way to address these matters. For example, DOD stated that the department is in the final stages of approving an instruction on the U.S. Global Defense Posture Process that will document roles, responsibilities, and requirements for global posture planning for key OSD organizations, the Joint Staff, the military departments, and the combatant commands. The instruction will institutionalize the Global Posture Integration Team and Global Posture Executive Council to provide formal oversight of global posture management. Additionally, DOD is in the process of issuing a data call to the military departments and combatant commands to help determine the existing infrastructure costs at enduring overseas installations. Lastly, DOD stated that the Joint Staff issued supplemental Theater Posture Plan guidance to the combatant commands in February 2012, including standardized reporting criteria (e.g., estimated costs) for future posture initiatives. If they are fully implemented, we believe DOD's actions should meet the intent of our recommendation.

The department also provided a number of general and technical comments that we considered and incorporated, as appropriate. A complete copy of DODs written comments is reprinted in appendix II.

We are sending a copy of this report to the Secretary of Defense; the Secretary of the Navy; and the Secretary of the Army. In addition, the report is available at no charge on the GAO website at http://www.gao.gov.

If you or your staff have any questions about this report, please contact me at (404) 679-1816 or pendletonj@gao.gov. Contact points for our Offices of Congressional Relations and Public Affairs may be found on the last page of this report. GAO staff who made key contributions to this report are listed in appendix III.

John H. Pendleton
Director
Defense Capabilities and Management

Appendix I: Scope and Methodology

To determine the extent to which the Department of Defense (DOD) conducted analysis of costs and savings associated with recent overseas posture decisions, we reviewed DOD documented cost data and collected additional information by interviewing officials associated with two major global force posture initiatives: the stationing of four Navy destroyers in Rota, Spain, to provide ballistic missile defense for the region and the reduction of permanently stationed Army forces in Europe. To determine the extent to which DOD conducted analysis to support the decision to station four Navy destroyers in Rota, Spain, we analyzed key documents and briefings provided by the U.S. Navy, U.S. European Command, and Naval Station Rota in order to assess assumptions, courses of action considered, and cost estimates. We conducted a site visit to Naval Station Rota to observe existing capabilities and needs for military construction projects identified by the Navy. We also collected information by interviewing officials from the U.S. Navy, Office of the Chief of Naval Operations; U.S. European Command; U.S. Navy Europe; and Naval Station Rota. To determine the extent to which DOD conducted analysis to support force structure reduction of Army brigade combat teams in Europe, we reviewed key documents from U.S European Command and U.S. Army Europe describing the status of planned force structure changes in Europe, including the 2010 and 2011 theater posture plans for U.S. European Command's area of responsibility. We also collected information by interviewing officials from Office of the Secretary of Defense (OSD), OSD Cost Assessment and Program Evaluation; the Office of the Under Secretary of Defense for Policy; the Office of the Under Secretary of Defense (Comptroller); Department of the Army, Program Assessment and Evaluation Division; U.S. European Command; and U.S. Army Europe. We analyzed and assessed cost estimates for multiple courses of action associated with the number of brigade combat teams in Europe developed by the U.S. Army, Program Assessment and Evaluation Division, against GAO's cost estimating criteria to determine the extent to which Army analysts employed best practices when developing the estimates.

To determine the extent to which DOD developed a process for making decisions about global posture initiatives that aligns with strategy and considers costs, as well as efforts made by combatant commands to compile and report comprehensive cost data on existing global posture and new posture initiatives in their theater posture plans, we evaluated core global posture strategy documents; current and draft DOD guidance; and other documentation we collected through interviewing with officials from OSD, the Joint Staff, U.S. European Command and its three service component commands, U.S. Pacific Command, U.S. Africa Command, the four military service headquarters, OSD, OSD Cost Assessment and Program Evaluation, the Office of the Under Secretary of Defense for Policy, the Office of the Under Secretary of Defense (Comptroller), and the Office of Under Secretary of Defense for Acquisition, Technology and Logistics. To determine the extent to which DOD's global posture process includes a consideration of cost, we observed the Joint Staff's November 2011 Posture Review Seminar at which officials employed the Global Posture Initiative and Project Prioritization Process to rank posture initiatives identified in the combatant commands' respective theater posture plans. We also analyzed and evaluated theater posture plans from 2010 and 2011 for each combatant command to determine the extent to which the plans included comprehensive cost data for each posture initiative. To identify potential challenges associated with the combatant commands' directive to compile and report comprehensive cost data, we collected information through interviews with officials from U.S. European Command and its service component commands, U.S. Pacific Command, and U.S. Africa Command.

We conducted this performance audit between June 2011 and May 2012 in accordance with generally accepted government auditing standards. Those standards require that we plan and perform the audit to obtain sufficient, appropriate evidence to provide a reasonable basis for our findings and conclusions based on our audit objectives. We believe that the evidence obtained provides a reasonable basis for our findings and conclusions based on our audit objectives.

Appendix II: Comments from the Department of Defense

UNDER SECRETARY OF DEFENSE
2000 DEFENSE PENTAGON
WASHINGTON, DC 20301-2000

POLICY

MAY 2 9 2012

Mr. John Pendleton
Director, Defense Capabilities and Management
U.S. Government Accountability Office
Room 4440B
441 G Street, NW
Washington DC 20548

Dear Mr. Pendleton:

This is the Department of Defense's (DoD) response to the Government Accountability Office's (GAO) draft report, "FORCE STRUCTURE: Improved Cost Information and Analysis Needed to Guide Overseas Military Posture Decisions" – GAO Code 351619/ GAO-12-711.

The Department concurs with two recommendations and partially concurs with one. Clarification and further information are included for each recommendation on the accompanying pages.

We will work with DoD components to implement these recommendations, and we look forward to further dialogue with GAO on costing posture initiatives.

Sincerely,

James N. Miller
Acting

UNCLASSIFIED

GAO DRAFT REPORT – DATED April 2012
GAO CODE 351619 / GAO-12-711

Force Structure: Improved Cost Information and Analysis Needed to
Guide Overseas Military Posture Decisions

DEPARTMENT OF DEFENSE COMMENTS TO THE RECOMMENDATIONS

RECOMMENDATION 1: Direct the Secretary of the Navy to conduct a comprehensive analysis for each course of action the Navy has considered to address mission requirements for ballistic missile defense in the Mediterranean, that compares all options the Navy considered and either applies consistent operational assumptions or controls for different operational assumptions and includes the long-term life-cycle costs and annual operating costs associated with forward stationing.

DoD Response: Partial Concur. DoD agrees that analysis is required prior to posture decisions. DoD disagrees that additional analysis is required to evaluate ballistic missile defense requirements in the Mediterranean. The Navy conducted extensive analysis comparing options from both operational and cost perspectives. Calculations for one-time costs and recurring costs were integral elements of the analyses. The Navy is implementing the most cost effective option—forward basing ships in Rota—to provide ballistic missile defense and to meet the demand for large surface combatants' presence. The criteria used to assess each option included: the level of presence generated; strategic laydown and dispersal; training; port infrastructure; ship maintenance; personnel costs; quality of life; operational flexibility; and the number of ships required, and ship scheduling.

The Navy held the operational assumptions constant when comparing the options of forward basing ships in Rota and basing them stateside. These included the demand for large surface combatants, the West Coast distribution of ships, and the employment cycle for ships based stateside. To identify ship requirements without forward basing in Rota, the Navy assessed how many U.S.-based ships would be required to meet the presence level equivalent to that provided by Rota ships. The effect on force structure of not having ships in Rota would require an increase of 10 large surface combatants, requiring a one-time capital cost of $22B (constant FY12 dollars, outside of FYDP). The average yearly operations and maintenance cost for these ships stateside is $23M per ship. The average yearly operation and maintenance cost for ships in Rota is $30M per ship.

The Navy commissioned the Center for Naval Analysis to study the effects of rotational crewing, and the findings further support Navy's plan to forward base large surface combatants in Rota. Depending on the rotational crewing model and operational availability assumptions used, a crew rotation approach could require an additional two to twelve large surface combatants to support U.S. European Command (USEUCOM) demand in the Mediterranean. This corresponds to a one-time capital cost of $4B-$27B (constant FY12 dollars, outside of FYDP). Ship operations and maintenance costs were estimated to be similar to the operations and maintenance costs for ships with a non-rotational crewing scheme.

A concern with rotational crewing is increased stress on the crews. Rotated crews deploy multiple times during their employment cycle and swap ships numerous times, even while in

1

UNCLASSIFIED

their homeport. An additional concern is the negative impact of a ship not being "owned" by a single crew.

The decision to establish a Forward-Deployed Naval Force (FDNF) consisting of four BMD-capable multi-mission Aegis destroyers to Europe also took into consideration the increasing global demand for these assets. In Rota, Spain circumstances permit a cost-effective FDNF, making it a sound alternative to employing U.S. based rotational forces or rotational crewing. A FDNF in Rota is the most effective and efficient means to deliver sea-based BMD-capability to USEUCOM and it provides the greatest degree of operational responsiveness and flexibility.

RECOMMENDATION 2: Direct the Secretary of the Army to identify and assess options to rotate forces in Europe and their associated costs, including the impacts on future basing in Europe.

DoD Response: Concur. Army is currently working with USEUCOM and various Army components to identify and assess options for rotating personnel and equipment through Europe for training and exercises with allies and partners.

RECOMMENDATION 3: Clarify the roles and responsibilities of key DOD organizations such as Cost Assessment and Program Evaluation, the military departments, and the service component commands, and establish a standardized reporting format to include in applicable guidance for key DOD organizations to use to ensure that cost information is consistently summarized and reported to inform the posture planning process.

DoD Response: Concur. The Department is in the final stages of approving a Department of Defense Instruction (DoDI) on U.S. Global Defense Posture Process, which will document roles, responsibilities and requirements for global posture planning for OSD, the Joint Staff, the Military Departments, and the Combatant Commands. This DoDI institutionalizes the Global Posture Integration Team and Global Posture Executive Council to provide formal oversight of global posture management. Additionally, the Department is issuing a data call to the Military Departments and Combatant Commands to determine the existing infrastructure costs at enduring overseas installations. Lastly, the Joint Staff issued supplemental Theater Posture Plan guidance to the Combatant Commands in February 2012, including standardized reporting criteria (*e.g.*, estimated costs) for future posture initiatives.

2

Appendix III: GAO Contact and Staff Acknowledgments

GAO Contact	John H. Pendleton, (404) 679-1816 or pendletonj@gao.gov
Staff Acknowledgments	In addition to the contact named above, Guy LoFaro, Assistant Director; Robert L. Repasky, Assistant Director; Jennifer Echard; Joanne Landesman; Stephanie Moriarty; Charles Perdue; Carol Petersen; Courtney Reid, Analyst in Charge; Michael Shaughnessy; and Grant Sutton made key contributions to this report.

Related GAO Products

Defense Management: Additional Cost Information and Stakeholder Input Needed to Assess Military Posture in Europe. GAO-11-131. Washington, D.C.: February 3, 2011.

Defense Planning: DOD Needs to Review the Costs and Benefits of Basing Alternatives for Army Forces in Europe. GAO-10-745R. Washington, D.C.: September 13, 2010.

Defense Infrastructure: Guam Needs Timely Information from DOD to Meet Challenges in Planning and Financing Off-Base Projects and Programs to Support a Larger Military Presence. GAO-10-90R. Washington, D.C.: November 13, 2009.

Ballistic Missile Defense: Actions Needed to Improve Planning and Information on Construction and Support Costs for Proposed European Sites. GAO-09-771. Washington, D.C.: August 6, 2009.

Force Structure: Actions Needed to Improve DOD's Ability to Manage, Assess, and Report on Global Defense Posture Initiatives. GAO-09-706R. Washington, D.C.: July 2, 2009.

Defense Logistics: Navy Needs to Develop and Implement a Plan to Ensure That Voyage Repairs Are Available to Ships Operating near Guam when Needed. GAO-08-427. Washington, D.C.: May 12, 2008.

Defense Infrastructure: Challenges Increase Risks for Providing Timely Infrastructure Support for Army Installations Expecting Substantial Personnel Growth. GAO-07-1007. Washington, D.C.: September 13, 2007.

Defense Infrastructure: Overseas Master Plans Are Improving, but DOD Needs to Provide Congress Additional Information about the Military Buildup on Guam. GAO-07-1015. Washington, D.C.: September 12, 2007.

Defense Management: Comprehensive Strategy and Annual Reporting Are Needed to Measure Progress and Costs of DOD's Global Posture Restructuring. GAO-06-852. Washington, D.C.: September 13, 2006.

Opportunities Exist to Improve Future Comprehensive Master Plans for Changing U.S. Defense Infrastructure Overseas. GAO-05-680R. Washington, D.C.: June 27, 2005.

GAO's Mission	The Government Accountability Office, the audit, evaluation, and investigative arm of Congress, exists to support Congress in meeting its constitutional responsibilities and to help improve the performance and accountability of the federal government for the American people. GAO examines the use of public funds; evaluates federal programs and policies; and provides analyses, recommendations, and other assistance to help Congress make informed oversight, policy, and funding decisions. GAO's commitment to good government is reflected in its core values of accountability, integrity, and reliability.
Obtaining Copies of GAO Reports and Testimony	The fastest and easiest way to obtain copies of GAO documents at no cost is through GAO's website (www.gao.gov). Each weekday afternoon, GAO posts on its website newly released reports, testimony, and correspondence. To have GAO e-mail you a list of newly posted products, go to www.gao.gov and select "E-mail Updates."
Order by Phone	The price of each GAO publication reflects GAO's actual cost of production and distribution and depends on the number of pages in the publication and whether the publication is printed in color or black and white. Pricing and ordering information is posted on GAO's website, http://www.gao.gov/ordering.htm. Place orders by calling (202) 512-6000, toll free (866) 801-7077, or TDD (202) 512-2537. Orders may be paid for using American Express, Discover Card, MasterCard, Visa, check, or money order. Call for additional information.
Connect with GAO	Connect with GAO on Facebook, Flickr, Twitter, and YouTube. Subscribe to our RSS Feeds or E-mail Updates. Listen to our Podcasts. Visit GAO on the web at www.gao.gov.
To Report Fraud, Waste, and Abuse in Federal Programs	Contact: Website: www.gao.gov/fraudnet/fraudnet.htm E-mail: fraudnet@gao.gov Automated answering system: (800) 424-5454 or (202) 512-7470
Congressional Relations	Katherine Siggerud, Managing Director, siggerudk@gao.gov, (202) 512-4400, U.S. Government Accountability Office, 441 G Street NW, Room 7125, Washington, DC 20548
Public Affairs	Chuck Young, Managing Director, youngc1@gao.gov, (202) 512-4800 U.S. Government Accountability Office, 441 G Street NW, Room 7149 Washington, DC 20548

Please Print on Recycled Paper.

www.ingramcontent.com/pod-product-compliance
Lightning Source LLC
Chambersburg PA
CBHW080732290526

45790CB00008B/3166

* 9 7 8 1 4 9 0 4 7 8 4 5 6 *